WHY ME?

By the same author

Why Believe?
  The author of *Why Me?* looks at some evidence
  for Christian belief

WHY ME?

The author of *Why Believe?* looks at the
problem of suffering

Roger Carswell

Authentic

LONDON • COLORADO SPRINGS • HYDERABAD

First published 1993
Reprinted 1994, 1996, 1998, 2000, 2004 (2), 2007

13 12 11 10 09 08 07   14 13 12 11 10 9 8

Authentic Media, 9 Holdom Avenue, Bletchley, Milton Keynes,
Bucks., MK1 1QR
1820 Jet Stream Drive, Colorado Springs, CO 80921, USA
OM Authentic Media, Medchal Road, Jeedimetla Village, Secunderabad
500 055, A.P., India www.authenticmedia.co.uk
Authentic Media is a division of IBS-STL U.K., limited by guarantee,
with its Registered Office at Kingstown Broadway, Carlisle,
Cumbria CA3 0HA. Registered in England & Wales No. 1216232.
Registered charity 270162

British Library Cataloguing in Publication Data
A catalogue record for this book is available from the
British Library

ISBN-13: 978-1-85078-133-2

Cover Design by Diane Bainbridge
Typeset by Photoprint, Torquay, Devon
Printed in Great Britain by Cox and Wyman, Reading

Contents

Dedication

*To some very special and valued friends whose
stories do not appear in this book but who have
been able to comfort those who are in any
trouble with the comfort with which they themselves were comforted by God.*

(2 Corinthians 1:4-5)

1

Why Doesn't God Intervene?

I had been waiting for some time at the Czecho-
slovakian border for customs control to allow me
through into Austria. It was a beautiful, sunny
morning but the gentleman in the car behind me
looked gloomy and concerned. Eventually we
struck up a conversation.

He was a German university lecturer and, like
me, he was returning from Poland; but he had
visited Auschwitz, that memorial to the unimagin-
able suffering of the nineteen thirties and forties.
He felt overwhelmed with grief and shame.
Although he was a Christian he found himself
asking, as so many others did, 'Why didn't God do
something about it?'

Over many centuries suffering has afflicted
multitudes of people. It is just decades ago that six
million Jews were exterminated in the Holocaust,
but there have been other holocausts in our own
century. First, it was the Armenians who suffered
a similar fate. Since then, in more recent years,

between twenty and fifty million Chinese died under the rule of Chairman Mao. Millions of Soviet citizens died under the rule of Stalin; and names like Pol Pot, Idi Amin, Nicolae Ceausescu and Saddam Hussein strike terror into the hearts of bereft, beleaguered people.

The immediate causes of these and some other tragedies are clear. Human greed desires power, wealth or territory which in turn often leads to war which can produce so-called 'natural disasters'. Human negligence can result in a fatal train crash. A corrupt system of government will stop at nothing to eradicate those it perceives as enemies of the State.

But there are also apparently inexplicable tragedies. There are disasters which occur on a global or national scale. For a period the world media focuses attention on such tragedies, and compassion is aroused in the hearts of many. Debate and discussion follow with a view to preventing a recurrence of such disasters.

Despite this they continue to happen. Each year thousands die of starvation and millions suffer from malnutrition. We hear of masses dying in natural disasters such as earthquakes, famines, cyclones, droughts and rampant diseases.

Very often the pictures we see of the victims of such disasters concentrate on the individual. We see the solitary child with his bloated belly and his wasted limbs. We see the hopeless family surveying the home and the land overwhelmed by floods. In such ways we are reminded that communal disasters are, in fact, individual disasters.

Such individual disasters can indeed be found nearer home. They largely pass unnoticed by the world media; but bereavement, the break-up of a marriage, the rebellion of a child, financial ruin or even job disappointment have the power to wound deeply. Shattered dreams, disappointed hopes, broken hearts, as well as the problems of disease or old age, are close to all of us. It may be hard to enter into someone else's suffering when our own seems more than we can cope with. We may feel like my eight-year-old son who, when he heard what I was writing about, asked, 'Will you tell them about what happened when I went over the handlebars of my bike?'

Whether it comes as the result of international disaster or through personal tragedy, no suffering is trivial. It is, therefore, natural that people should ask, 'Why doesn't God intervene?' However, when we ask a question like this the inference appears to be that all this suffering is somehow God's responsibility, that it is part and parcel of the world that he created. This is far from the truth. The first chapters of the Bible show us clearly

The world as it was

The mighty God created the world in which we live. At the end of each day of creation he looked and saw that it was good. Six times we read in Genesis chapter 1 that what God had made was good. When the first man and woman had been created we read:'God saw all that he had made, and it was very good' (Gen 1:31).

It is impossible for us to imagine a world where there was no suffering, sin, disease or death. God created a paradise in which men and women could live in harmony with each other and with him. Everything in the universe was still supremely good. There was no struggle for existence, no environmental pollution, no physical calamities, no tears shed in uncontrolled hurt. Instead, there was a sense of total freedom, exhilaration, joy and peace.

Clearly something has gone wrong. Sin and death have entered the world and the results have been cataclysmic. The world as it was has become

The world as it is

In a moment of time, by an act of deliberate rebellion, the first man and woman disobeyed their Creator, opening the door for evil to flood the world. It was not God's intention that we should discover evil in the world, but when we did everything was affected. A curse came upon the creation affecting animals, women, men and the elements themselves. The stage was now set for the long, sad history of humanity. Things created for our benefit became instruments of blight.

The Bible shows us how all creation is involved in this suffering (Rom 8:22). A basic law of science, 'the Second Law of Thermodynamics' states that all systems left to themselves tend to become disordered. Such is our world today.

Human beings caught up in this world order are now born to suffering and eventually to death. Peter Marshall, a former chaplain to the US Senate used to tell this story: 'A merchant in Baghdad one day sent his servant to the market. Before very long the servant came back, pale and trembling. In great agitation he said to his master, "Down in the market-place I was jostled by a woman in the crowd, and when I turned around I saw it was Death. She looked at me and made a threatening gesture. Master, please lend me your horse, for I must hasten to avoid her. I will ride to Samarra and there I will hide, and Death will not find me." The merchant lent him his horse, and the servant galloped away in great haste.

Later the merchant went down to the market and saw Death standing in the crowd. He asked her, "Why did you frighten my servant this morning? Why did you make a threatening gesture?"

"That was not a threatening gesture," Death said. "It was only a start of surprise. I was astonished to see him in Baghdad, for I have an appointment with him tonight in Samarra." '

Louis Armstrong may sing about 'a wonderful world' but we know that all is not well. Instead we hear about trouble in the Middle East, in Africa, in Belfast or Beirut, or disaster in Aberfan or Armenia, in Bangladesh or Baghdad, in the Sudan or South Africa.

So when we ask why God allows suffering we have to face the fact that it is basically the result of man's own sin. Sometimes it is even the direct result. The God who is love is also a just God who must punish sin. Sometimes that punishment seems to be withheld, even until after death, but at other times it is more immediate. In the Bible we read of how God judged nations, cities and individuals because of their continued refusal to obey his commands. If people flout God's laws, then somewhere along the line will be suffering on a personal or communal scale. Everything we do has a consequence.

However, although all suffering is the indirect result of human rebellion against God this does not mean that some particular incident is the result of a particular sin.

In John chapter 9, Jesus was asked whether the sin of a blind man's parents or of the man himself had led to his blindness. Jesus replied that it was neither of these that had brought about blindness. The blind man was bound up in the bundle of life, but Jesus also said that God would be glorified through it all.

The Bible also teaches us that the world will not always be torn apart by sin, suffering and strife. It points us to

The world as it will be

As it looks into the future the Bible teaches us that the present troubles are in themselves a sign of the future time when Christ will return to this earth, not as a baby in a manger, but as king of kings and bringing judgment on all who do not know him as Lord and Saviour. Many Christians believe that that day may be imminent.

The story is told of a child who heard the town hall clock chime the hour. It struck not twelve times but thirteen. The child ran to his mother and said: 'Mummy, it is later than it has ever been before.' That is how our present times seem to some Christians.

In 2 Timothy 3 Paul wrote: 'There will be terrible times in the last days. People will be lovers of themselves, lovers or money, boastful, proud, abusive, disobedient to their parents, ungrateful, unholy, without love, unforgiving, slanderous, without self-control, brutal, not lovers of the good, treacherous, rash, conceited, lovers of pleasure rather than lovers of God — having a form of godliness but denying its power . . . always learning but never able to acknowledge the truth.'

In Matthew 24 Jesus said that some of the signs indicating the build up to the last days would be many coming in his name saying, 'I am the Christ.' There would be wars and rumours of wars, famines, earthquakes and persecutions, false prophets showing signs and wonders, lawlessness and then great tribulation. The decadence of this present age is foretold in the Bible and is one of the signs that the coming of the Lord Jesus is getting nearer.

We also learn from the Bible that one day an eternal sentence will be passed on certain people. Gravestones often have engraved upon them the letters, RIP. But there will be no rest for those who persistently refuse to accept the one and only way of salvation which God has provided. Jesus who was so full of love consistently warned people of the necessity to turn from their sins and trust him as the only one who can forgive a person and be with them not only in this life but through eternity.

In the last book of the Bible, almost on the last page, God again underscores the everlasting penalty for those who refuse to receive God's mercy. 'The cowardly, the unbelieving, the vile, the murderers, the sexually immoral, those who practise magic arts, the idolaters and all liars — their place will be in the fiery lake of burning sulphur. This is the second death' (Rev 21:8).

For those who are 'in Christ' troubles will cease at the moment of death or at the return of Jesus Christ. The Christian looks forward to the time when 'God will wipe every tear from their eyes. There will be no more death, nor sorrow nor crying. There will be no more pain for the former things have passed away' (Rev 21:4).

The paradise lost when sin entered the world will be a paradise regained. We read in the Bible of a new heaven and a new earth. Heaven is home for all those who know Christ. Their place has been purchased at the price of the blood of Christ. His death for sin is God's only means whereby the passport to heaven can be given to all those who will receive it. The journey may not always be smooth but the final outcome is glorious.

2

God Intervenes – To His Own Cost
Introduction

The world's oldest book is believed by many people to be the Book of Job. Lord Tennyson called it 'the greatest poem, whether of ancient or modern literature'. It is fitting that the oldest book should deal with the oldest of problems — 'Why do the innocent suffer?'

The book opens with a scene in heaven where Satan, the supreme cynic, suggests to God himself that Job fears God only because of the material prosperity that results from his devotion. Job never knew of this conversation, but in reply God allowed Satan to take from Job his children, his business and even his health. Bereft, bankrupt and covered with boils, even Job's wife appeared to turn against him.

In all Job's dire sufferings he never accused God of wrongdoing. In fact he said, 'Naked I came from my mother's womb and naked I shall depart. The Lord gave and the Lord has taken away; may the name of the Lord be praised' (Job 1:21).

However, so dark was his experience and so vain were the words of his so-called 'comforters' that Job grappled with words and metaphors to try to express the anguish of his soul.

In chapter 19 of his book he likened himself to an animal caught in a net (v 6); to a criminal in court (v 7); to a traveller stuck in a roadblock (v 8); to a dethroned king (v 9); to a building which is being demolished and to a tree being uprooted (v 10); to an enemy being besieged by God (vv 11–12). He describes emotionally how his relatives and friends, servants and children forsook and persecuted him.

Perhaps you find yourself identifying with Job. Maybe life is treating you harshly. Nobody understands you, and least of all can you understand yourself. So is there any clear answer as to why God allows us to suffer?

We have to admit at the outset that there are some questions to which we do not yet know the answers. It is significant that although we know the background to Job's story he was never told why he had to endure such affliction.

Down through the centuries Christians have come face to face with the same problem. John Paton who was a missionary in the New Hebrides, had to dig the graves both of his only son and of his wife. He wrote in his journal in 1859: 'I do not pretend to see through the mystery of such visitations, but I do know that God is my Father.'

Nearer to our own time is the experience of Dr Helen Roseveare. As a medical missionary working in the Belgian Congo at the time of the Simba rebellion in 1964, she was brutally treated, raped and imprisoned. She has since asked Christians: 'Do you trust God enough to allow him to allow you to suffer if he never tells you why?'

We have already seen how individuals suffer from deliberate acts and also from negligence. Events at Lockerbie, in Armenia and Enniskillen, the tragedies of Zeebrugge, Hillsborough, Belfast and King's Cross, all bear witness to this.

Nearly two thousand years ago two similar incidents were the subject of comment by the Lord Jesus Christ. In the first, in a deliberate act of official terrorism Galileans were massacred in the Temple while worshipping God. This was a religious and political atrocity ordered by Pilate, the Roman governor who had been put in charge of Judea. It was a foolish act and helped to bring about Pilate's final downfall, but that did not help the people who were martyred in this act of violence. In the second incident eighteen people died when the Tower of Siloam collapsed. Whether this was through poor design or wrong construction or use of the building we can only guess. Despite the passing of years the Bible is always relevant and topical.

Luke records how people brought to Jesus the news of Pilate's massacre of the pilgrims. In reply Jesus draws two lessons and links the two incidents. The first lesson was that in neither case was it the 'guilty' who had suffered. It was the sinfulness, the cruelty of Pilate which led to the first tragedy. Nobody can tell who was responsible for the second. The victims, like the blind man of

John chapter 9, were caught up in the bundle of life. They were neither more innocent nor more guilty than those around them.

The second lesson that Jesus drew from the incidents was that they call us to repentence. 'Unless you repent, you too will all perish' (Lk 13:5). The theme of repentance runs through the whole Bible. It was when the people of Nineveh repented at the preaching of Jonah that God spared the city. Repentance was the great theme of the preaching of John the Baptist. It was at the heart of Peter's message on the Day of Pentecost. In all his recorded sermons Paul called upon his hearers to repent. The same message comes to us all today. We all need to repent of our sins. Each individual needs to turn deliberately from sin and towards Christ.

It is God himself that has made such a turning and a salvation possible. He did this when he seemed to stand aside from an evil situation and yet, at the same time, made that situation the greatest act of divine intervention. Have you ever wondered why, when his own Son was being crucified, God did not appear to intervene?

God had already stepped into the world he had created. He had been born not in a mansion, but in a manger, the son of a young virgin who was not yet married. Throughout Christ's three years of earthly ministry he was scorned and derided. While he went about doing good, bringing speech to the dumb, sight to the blind, hearing to the deaf, cleansing to the leper, strength to the lame, life to the dead and forgiveness to the sinner, his enemies were plotting to kill him. At the end the mob howled for his crucifixion.

Christ suffered physically

His back was beaten with many lashings; they spat in his face, beat and buffeted him, plucked his beard from his face, pushed a crown of thorns down upon his head and then on his lacerated back made him carry a rough, rugged, Roman cross. At Calvary they nailed his hands and feet to the cross, leaving him to hang naked in the scorching heat in agony, blood and sweat.

Christ suffered emotionally

His disciples who had once forsaken everything to follow him, now forsook him and fled. Crowds who had heard the finest of messages, who had been fed by his hand and healed by him, now mocked him and left him to die.

Christ suffered spiritually

Throughout all eternity-past Jesus had been at one with his Father. The Father, Son and Holy Spirit had experienced perfect unity and love — one God in three persons: three in one. Yet now Christ cried out, 'My God, my God, why have you forsaken me?'

Christians throughout the centuries have experienced the immediate presence of God. As his enemies put him on trial before stoning him to death, Stephen looked up to see Christ standing in heaven waiting to receive him. Paul, the great

missionary, near the time of his execution wrote:
'At my first defence, no-one came to my support
but everyone deserted me . . . But the Lord stood
at my side and gave me strength' (2 Tim 4:16-17).

By contrast Christ on the cross had no sense of
the presence of his Father. God laid on him the sin
of a lost world. The evil, the wrong thoughts and
deeds that had brought so much suffering into the
world were laid on Jesus Christ. It was for this
reason that the Father turned away from his own
Son as Christ the pure and holy one endured the
trauma of bearing our sin. This had to happen
because he was dying to purchase forgiveness for
all who will turn to him. Sin separates, so Jesus
endured separation for us. Sin brings death and
hell, so Jesus endured our hell and died. As a song
says, 'He could have called ten thousand angels to
set him free . . . but he died alone for you and me.'

We can never plumb the depths that Jesus went
through for us. To be cut off from his Father, to
carry our sins and to die, are experiences deeper
and darker than any other individual has ever had
to go through. God the Father allowed his Son to
suffer all this because there was no other way for
sinful people like you and me to receive forgiveness and be reconciled to God. Calvary is the place
where God did intervene at the cost of tremendous
suffering to himself.

While 'Good Friday' reminds us of the death of
Christ we also have Easter Sunday. The death of
Jesus was not the end of the story. He rose from
the dead, having conquered sin and the grave. He
had defeated the root cause of all the trouble in the

world. He can overcome the despair that people feel.

Because of what Jesus Christ has done for us on the cross we are rescued from the terrible feelings expressed by Job, which we listed earlier.

He spoke of feeling trapped, but when a person trusts Jesus Christ as Lord and Saviour he is set free. Jesus said, 'If the Son sets you free, you will be free indeed' (Jn 8:36).

Job thought of himself as a criminal, but Paul could write of the Christian. 'There is therefore now no condemnation for those who are in Christ Jesus' (Rom 8:1).

The believer need never feel that he is in a roadblock. Instead he is guided all along the way. 'The Lord guides a man in the way he should go' (Ps 37:23). Instead of feeling like a dethroned king, those who receive Christ have a new power, the power to do right. 'You have made us kings and priests to our God' (Rev 5:10).

As soon as a believer has accepted Jesus Christ as Saviour and Lord, God by his Holy Spirit comes to live in that person. Job thought of himself as a building being destroyed and as an uprooted tree; but the experience of the Christian is that while the body may grow weak and weary, the soul is being renewed (2 Cor 4:16).

Job felt that God had become his enemy but all who repent and believe are reconciled to God through Jesus Christ (Rom 5:10).

Job felt isolated, but God promises his eternal presence with us when we trust him. The believer can echo the words of the Psalmist: 'When my

mother and father forsake me the Lord will take
care of me' (Ps 27:10).

The death of Jesus was seen at first by his
disciples to be a catastrophe of untold proportions.
But when Jesus rose from the dead they realized
that this seeming tragedy was in fact God's major
triumph, one in which all those who put their trust
in him can share.

The death of Jesus is an unforgettable event.
Human tragedies pass from our minds, but the
death of Jesus will never be forgotten.

Christians meet regularly to eat bread and drink
wine as a deliberate reminder of the fact that Jesus
died for us. His body was broken; his blood was
shed to buy for us forgiveness and new life. We can
never forget such a sacrifice, never forget that God
has intervened at such tremendous cost to himself.

Introduction

We have already seen that being a Christian is no
guarantee of trouble-free living. For nearly two
thousand years true believers have suffered both
physically and mentally, because of natural
disasters, or disease, or at the hands of evil people
who have persecuted and martyred the followers
of Christ.

The world that hated Jesus has often hated his
followers. It is reckoned that the 20th century has
had more Christian martyrs than the previous
nineteen added together. There are still countries
where Christians are hounded, imprisoned and
even killed. Believers are not immunized against

the suffering of a world where the innocent are often caught up in the consequences of others' guilt.

Christianity is more than a crutch (though a crutch can be very useful!). God promises to be an ever present help in time of trouble (Ps 46:1). He is well able to meet the deepest needs of any individual. He is never caught out or taken by surprise by events.

Christ spent his life bringing help to those in need. He gave sight to the blind, hearing to the deaf, speech to the dumb, strength to the lame, cleansing to the leper and life to the dead. However, he did not bring healing to all those whom he met. On one occasion Jesus went to the pool of Bethesda. There out of 'a great multitude' he healed one paralyzed man. We cannot explain why Jesus healed some people but not others. We know that all power is his and that he has perfect wisdom.

There is a Bible verse which has brought hope and comfort to countless Christians across the years. 'And we know that all things work together for good to those who love God, to those who are called according to his purpose' (Rom 8:28). To believe this is not to clutch at straws. It is the result of the Christian experience of those who rest upon what God has promised in his Word.

In the following chapters are eight stories of people from different parts of the United Kingdom, all Christians who in different and often dramatic ways, have suffered and are still suffering. All the stories are true in every detail. All the people involved are still alive.

Two themes shine through the darkness of their experiences.

1. They have an overwhelming sense of God's presence with them despite everything.
2. They have an unshakeable confidence and trust that God has a purpose in all that has happened, even though at present they may not know or understand it.

3

Back From 'The Dead'
The Story of Sara Edwards

Fear not, for I am with you; be not dismayed, for I am your God. I will strengthen you, yes, I will help you. I will uphold you with my righteous right hand.
(Isa 41:10)

'One perfect day last summer, I walked along a quiet path near my Welsh home. It was a path I had run along as a child. Now, I had to take it more slowly with the help of a walking stick. Yet, as I gazed up at the mountains, I thanked God I could walk at all. At eighteen, I'd contracted a severe form of meningitis and both my legs had been amputated. Now I felt I had finally made it back from a long and frightening journey.' So says Sara Edwards.

Sara was born in August 1968 in Wales. Both she and her parents are fluent Welsh speakers. She was a bright girl who always wanted to be a doctor. At the age of fifteen she passed twelve 'O' levels, and two years later she was taking her 'A' levels. However, the night before the first examination, she suffered a slipped disc and ended up actually taking her 'A' level examinations on her back with an external examiner sitting in. The fact that Liverpool University Medical School accepted her was proof to her that the Lord wanted her there. This was the first real drama of her life. Until then Sara was just a normal healthy girl enjoying cycling, swimming and squash. It was at a Christian camp that Sara had become a real Christian. Recalling what happened, she says that she trusted Christ as a fourteen year old:

'It was the first time that I had really heard the gospel and realized that I was a sinner. I always thought that because I lived in a so-called Christian country, said the Lord's Prayer before I went to bed, tried to get my homework in on time, and did not lie or steal, I was a Christian. Then at that camp I heard about heaven and hell, I learned that I needed to be "born again" so that Christ would become a reality in my life, and I could enjoy personal relationship with God. As a young girl it really frightened me and made me realize that I was going to hell. But the message about Jesus the Saviour, and a loving God who sent his Son to die for all of us at Calvary reassured me. Understanding that Jesus loved me as I was, and had taken the punishment for my sins on the cross gave me such joy and security. I prayed a prayer that night asking Jesus to come into my life, to forgive my sins, and to take control of me to make me whatever he wanted me to be. The following morning I told the leader of the camp about it. I can remember asking everyone to sing the chorus, "I have decided to follow Jesus". That really became my sort of motto, and there was no turning back.'

Sara remembers talking to a Christian friend at Liverpool University and saying, 'I don't know why the Lord has brought me to Liverpool, but I know there is a reason for it.' She has often been reminded of that since, believing that the reason was revealed when she became ill. What happened next she tells us in her own words.

'I was very excited when I went to University. It was a new chapter in my life, with independence from home, being my own person, developing my own character. I had to stand on my own two feet, and start taking responsibility for my actions, being organized and planning my life. I felt I had to stand as a Christian since there were so many temptations around. Everybody else was living their own lives and going to pubs and discos, so it took me a while really to work out where I wanted to go and whether I wanted to give in totally to God. One thing I found excellent while I was there was that I could go into so many churches in Liverpool and hear the gospel, because at home we had to travel some way to find a gospel-believing church. On the Sunday before I became ill, I can remember walking down a road and seeing a road sign saying, "Change priorities ahead", and it made a real impression on me. I knew that even though I was trying my best to live a Christian life and to honour the Lord, there was something

wrong and I was just holding back that little bit. It
was as if God was saying to me, "No, you have to
give in completely to me". Seeing that sign made
me realize that God has to be first and I have to give
him one hundred per cent. That night I sincerely
prayed that God would change me and make me
the person that he would have me be. I wanted to
be more useful to him. I never thought when I
prayed that particular prayer how he would
change me and how dramatic the outward change
would be. It was the following Wednesday that I
was taken ill.

'I had had a good day at the university. I had an
exam on the Thursday so I was working hard that
night. I 'phoned home and told my mum I had a
slight sore throat but during the night the sore
throat became worse. I started vomiting and
gradually became more and more ill. I was taken to
the university sick bay and eventually that night
the doctor came and diagnosed meningitis. I was
rushed to an infectious diseases hospital in
Liverpool. I arrived there and subsequently had
two cardiac arrests. So I suppose theoretically I
died twice. But they resuscitated me. My parents
were called from Wales. It must have been a
terrible shock to them when the doctor said,
"Your daughter is seriously ill and we think she
might even be dying. Can you get over here as
quickly as possible?" They naturally came straight
away, and that night I just seemed to grow weaker.

I was very aware of what was happening and my
mum often tells me that I would swing my legs
over the bed and bang them on the floor. I kept on

saying, "Rub my legs, rub my legs, I can feel the blood clotting." Even though my parents were told when they arrived that I had perhaps about half an hour to live, I managed miraculously to survive that night. The following day I went into respiratory failure and needed a life support machine, so I was transferred to the Intensive Care Unit of another hospital. I remained on the life support machine for over six weeks. I stayed in that hospital for two days, but then my kidneys failed and I needed dialysis equipment so I was transferred to yet another hospital to be put on a dialysis machine. My liver then failed and everything seemed hopeless. My condition just deteriorated. The doctors said the situation was hopeless and ten days into my illness they decided, as a last resort, to amputate both my legs below the knee.

'I was in a coma at this time and it seemed that my life was just hanging by a thread, but I know that God was in control. When I became a Christian he promised me never to leave me nor forsake me. He was in control of my life and had a specific plan for it, and even when I was on that life support machine and everyone had given up hope, and the situation seemed so, so hopeless, he was there and sustained me and was in control. Thousands of God's people prayed and I really believe that it is by God's grace and the power of prayer that I am here today.

'I came round six weeks later to discover that I no longer had any feet and at that time, because of the drugs I was on, my memory was very poor, so they had to keep on telling me that I had lost my legs. Then one night, in the middle of the night, it really dawned on me what had happened. My parents had gone home for a couple of hours' sleep, so I asked the nurse to call them. They came, and I actually told them then what had happened, that I had lost my legs. It seemed as if it was my way of coping with it. I cannot deny it was a shock but I was so thankful to be alive. I realized how ill I had been and God was so real to me in that Intensive Care Unit. It was as if Jesus was there, standing at the end of the bed, whenever I was lonely and desperate or worried about the future and asking whether I would ever walk again. He gave me the peace that I needed, and I became thankful for little things and appreciated life for what it was. Things like being able to keep some food down, or eating jelly became such a blessing in a way. I think that has really taught me that in our lives from day to day we have to be thankful and must live one day at a time. A few weeks later I was taken down on to a general ward and I remained in hospital for seven months in all because I had to learn to walk again.

'Learning to walk on artificial legs is quite a long process and because I was very weak at the time, it was very hard. I had lost weight and was about 5½ stone then. But I just knew that I had to walk. If I wanted to be useful to God and to anyone again, I had to give it a go. It was very experimental in the first stages. I didn't decide, "Yes, I am going to walk again." It was, "Come on let's see if you can", and I can remember the first day they asked me to walk just a few steps. I actually walked about ten feet (which was such a distance), and then gradually day after day and week after week I became stronger and more able to walk. Eventually in the gym I was given a pair of legs that actually looked like legs, and I started walking with walking sticks. Even then God was with me and daily he gave me the strength and the courage to keep on going. He gave me, as well, the inner strength not to become bitter. Many things happened during that time in hospital. People said things that maybe they did not mean, but nevertheless that really upset me at the time. However, I still had a perspective that even though it was hard, this life is not for ever. God had kept me and would continue to keep me.'

Sara has a quiet confidence that even if she has to be on artificial legs for sixty or seventy years, ultimately it does not matter when compared with eternity and the certainty that heaven is her eternal home. The thought of being with Christ where there will be no more pain, trials or burdens to carry was what kept her going in the early days and does now.

Not everything was easy. One man receiving physiotherapy who had had amputations in exactly the same place said to her one day, 'Oh, who will marry you girl? Your dancing days are over, aren't they?' She was very fragile at that time, and just sat in her wheelchair, wheeled herself to the hospital chapel and wept. Even then, God undertook because there was a Christian doctor at the Royal whom she had never met before, but who came in just then. He was an older man and he put his arm around her and said, 'It's all right now, I'm here.' Sara says, 'It was so strange. It was as if the Lord was saying to me, "I'm here." ' She has not seen that doctor since, but that day he was a blessing and really helped.

When things get out of perspective now and little things become important, her remedy is a good cry, a good pray, and a good night's sleep. In that order! Sara had found that Satan knows when to get at a person. He knows when we are weak, and it is at those times we have to turn back to the Bible and to the fact that Christ died on the cross, and get life in perspective again, realizing that ultimately none of this matters. 'O.K. you've had a horrible day. O.K. your legs are hurting. O.K. things have been awful, but ultimately all that matters is that you are safe for eternity and that you are on your way home. It is only a matter of time and the Lord could come back tomorrow, and that is what we need to be ready for,' she says reassuringly.

At the time, there was national interest in Sara. The *Liverpool Echo*, the *Sunday Telegraph* and the *Sunday Times* and *Bella* magazine, as well as Welsh television told her story. She received many cards. Now time has passed. Since the illness, Sara has passed her driving test learning to drive with hand controls, she has returned to medical school and has completed her course, and she has artificial legs. 'I didn't have a clue what an artificial leg looked like and I was so scared at the prospect of wearing what I thought were just going to be big metal calipers. But a girl who was a fourth year medical student walked into the Intensive Care Unit and said, "I'm an amputee, can you tell which leg is mine and which is artificial?" I was worried about how I could get my tights on and off and just little things like that, and she knew and could explain. She really helped me during that time.'

On August 17th, 1991 Sara married Dave, a doctor. They met at the first Saturday night's Christian Union meeting in Liverpool University of her first year. She thought he was great, but a bit unattainable for her! But they got to know each other. He came and visited her and even when she was on a life support machine he used to go and look through the window. He really prayed and got the Christian Union to pray. He started visiting her more and more and they gradually became closer. On the first Sunday Sara was allowed out of hospital she wanted to go to church. She was still in her wheelchair and together with her family she went to their church where they put on a thanksgiving service because she was there, and David sang a solo. 'Like any other Christian couple, we can say the Lord put us together. I can look back on the past years and feel I would never have got this far if the Lord had not gone before and prepared the way for me. He has brought me thus far and he is not going to let me go now. He is the same yesterday, today and for ever, and no matter what may happen to us in the future we know that he is faithful because he has proved his love for us in that he died on Calvary. We should never ask him to prove his love for us again. I can say that he has proved his promises that he will

never leave me or forsake me. He is my God and he
is faithful. Jesus is a friend who sticks closer than a
brother and he will never let me down. He knows
exactly how I feel even when I feel at rock bottom.
It is then that he gives me all that I need. He gives
me the grace and the strength just to cope with the
situation. Most importantly we have this inner
life, and I am on my way to heaven and I am going
home. One day I am going to get there and I am
going to see my Saviour's face. Just seeing him and
the beauty of heaven is going to be worth all the
pain and suffering and the trials, and every tear I
have shed here on earth is just going to be wiped
away. Then I believe God is going to give me a new
set of legs and the best set of legs ever. I am going
to be able to do the things I have missed here like
running up and down stairs and things like that.
Ultimately I think I will be so taken up with him
that I won't want to do anything else. I think that
even if the Lord sat me down today and explained
why it all happened I would not be able to
understand. It is only then when I will be made
like him that I will understand, but then I won't
need the answers because I will just be so happy to
be there and it will all be worth it.'

4

A Shattered Family
The Story of Lucy

(Christian names have been changed in this story)

He heals the broken-hearted and binds up their wounds. (Ps 147:3)

Lucy was one of four children brought up in a non-Christian home. Her mother died when Lucy was twelve. As a child she had gone to church but Jesus was to her only a character of history.

When she was in her late teens, her father attended a mission held in their local church and one day he came home telling the children that he had been converted. This was the first real contact that Lucy had with the gospel. She noticed a new joy about her father. He even started singing hymns.

Lucy had got to know the daughter of the minister of this church and she too seemed to have

a personal knowledge of God. This girl knew
Christ not just as someone in the distant past but as
a real person. All this started Lucy thinking
seriously about the things of God.

Some time later Lucy herself went to a town-
wide mission where the evangelist spoke about the
danger of 'sitting on the fence'. By this time she
was very familiar with the gospel and knew that
she should trust Christ. Though she believed that
Christ loved her, and had even died to take her sin
on himself, she was still hesitant about taking what
seemed a huge step to her. But that evening she
prayed, thanking Christ for dying for her, and
asking the risen Jesus to come to live in her life. As
she left that meeting she thought, 'God is out here,
he is everywhere, but best of all, he is in me.' She
was seventeen years old.

Immediately she sensed a peace, knowing the
real presence of the Lord with her. She now
wanted to live to please God rather than just to live
for herself.

Having worked as a secretary for a while, Lucy
joined the police force at the age of nineteen. She
dealt mainly with children, young people and
women whilst working 'on the beat'. Later she
worked with the traffic police and in an accident
unit.

At the age of twenty one she had an accident in a
police car in a collision with a heavy goods vehicle.
As a result she suffered whiplash injuries. At this
time she did not even have time off work thinking
that nothing serious had happened.

During all this time Lucy's Christian convictions were growing stronger. She was involved in interdenominational Christian youth work and in her own church. She took six months' unpaid leave to go to Bible college. Upon her return she was transferred to another police station and it was here that she met Richard. They were on the same shift and in the course of duty got to know each other. She grew to like him but she did not want to get involved with a non-Christian. Since Christ was the most important part of her life and she wanted to obey the Lord's commands she could really share her life only with someone who had the same priorities.

In 1976 Richard went to an evangelistic mission held in a tent. There was no pressure to make a commitment, but Richard made a profession of faith in Christ as his Lord and Saviour. Lucy had stressed that she didn't want Richard to become a Christian just to please her, but as a genuine commitment. Eventually Richard and Lucy started courting and were married in 1977.

In 1979 Lucy started to have problems with walking. As she had not been born with any deformity of the back, the medical specialist traced the cause to the accident of some years earlier. She had an operation on her back, and as a result had to leave the Police. The Lord blessed her and her husband with two daughters.

Lucy still had difficulty in walking and things seemed to improve little, so she returned to the doctor who had performed the back operation. For the first time she was told the real trouble was that she had degenerative multiple sclerosis. At

last she felt she had been given a name to what
before had been just an unknown condition.
Knowing the reason why, helped to get things in
perspective for her. Her condition has gradually
worsened so that now she is unable to go out for
walks and what little mobility she has is with the
aid of sticks, though she is still able to drive.

But her situation was to worsen. After five years
of suffering with multiple sclerosis, when her
husband was working away during the week as a
police instructor, she began to notice that everything was not quite right with Richard. She
couldn't tell exactly what was wrong, but he
seemed to lose his closeness with the Lord,
although he was still going to church.

One night they were talking when out of the
blue Lucy said to him, 'What is troubling you?
. . . There isn't anyone else is there?' It was one of
those questions that you never know why you have
asked, never imagining what the real answer
would be. There was a pause and then Lucy
realized what the problem was.

They tried to talk things through, but Lucy was
shocked that a professing Christian should act like
this. Together they sought Christian advice but
Richard did not really want to talk to anyone and
did not want help. Although Richard had not
actually committed adultery, as the weeks passed
his relationship with the student policewoman
deepened. The marriage broke up as he left his
physically impaired wife and two daughters, who
feared lest Mum should leave as well.

The church has been very helpful. 'But the great

blessing for me,' says Lucy, 'is knowing that the Lord is with me. When Richard eventually left, I had a great peace. At first I thought, "How am I going to sort out everything? What will I do about finances? What about the house?" Yet I can honestly say that I had such a peace and assurance that the Lord was with me. That was the great thing which sustained me. I can remember thinking afterwards that if I got Richard back but did not have this peace with the Lord, I wouldn't want Richard back. The Lord has been such a comfort to me.

'Of course I have wondered, "Why?" I don't know what purpose the Lord has in it, but I am confident that he has a purpose and that he knows full well what he is doing. I believe God called Richard and me together. God does not make mistakes. I don't know the final outcome, but I at least know God, and he is in control.

'Spiritually my life is deeper; I have realized that my walk with the Lord is the most important part of my life. Even when I was feeling very hurt and Richard had told me that he didn't love me any more, I thought of the fact that God sent his only Son to die for me as he did for Richard. But now Richard has turned round and thrown God's love back in the Lord's face. So how must the Lord feel when he loved Richard so much that he died for him? It's not just me that's hurting, it is the Lord as well.'

5

Death of a 'Good Samaritan'
The Story of Richard Garnham

Even though I walk through the valley of the shadow of death, I will fear no evil; for you are with me; your rod and your staff, they comfort me. (Ps 23:4)

Richard Garnham had asked Christ to be his Lord and Saviour after being challenged in a metalwork room at school as to whether he was truly a Christian. He feared the prospect of hell if he were to die without trusting the Saviour. He knew that Christ was the only one who could forgive him and bring him to know God. He believed Christ had died and was risen. That night he knelt by his bedside and asked the Lord Jesus Christ to be his Saviour. He says that that night he had the best night's sleep because he had peace with God, and the peace of God in his heart.

On January 16, 1984 tragedy struck their family. Richard explains what happened.

'I belong to a very musical family. My dad was in the brass band. We always had a friendly argument because I was a great pipe band man. We did a lot of singing together as a family, and also my mum and dad went out to different churches all over Northern Ireland singing together to the glory of the Lord. Often the entire family of two boys and two girls would join them. We had many good times singing together in the home. We were always looked upon as a singing family with musical talent. On the 16th January, 1984, there was a real tragedy for my family.

'It was a very cold and windy day. Snow was lying on the ground as I made my way to work. I worked in Dromara — miles away from my home — as a body builder (cars!). I tried to get there but couldn't as my car was sliding dangerously in the snow.

'I returned home and was idly hanging about town when I saw the Fire Brigade return from a call. As a Fire Officer, my father had just co-ordinated the rescue of two ambulancemen trapped in their vehicle by a fallen tree. Shortly after, the Fire Brigade was called out again to a similar accident where a tree had fallen on a car. This time I followed the Fire Engine with its gripping chains on the wheels and bells jangling — a sound I've always loved.

'The Fire Brigade were trying to contact my father but this time there was no reply from his call signal, "Bravo 1–3" for my father was dead and they were trying to get him to go to his own accident.

'As we approached a corner, 200 yards from the accident, I was prevented from going any further by another fallen tree. I believe this to have been the Lord's intervention to shield me from what would have been an unforgettable experience.

'I headed for home, expecting my father to pass me in his command car on his way to the accident. At home my mum asked me if I had seen my dad because headquarters were looking for him. I said, "No," and sat down to prepare my Sunday School lesson.

'Later, there was a knock on the door and two black figures stood there. I looked and thought it was my father coming home and bringing somebody with him for dinner as he did sometimes. However, one was the chief fire officer of Northern Ireland and the other his deputy. As soon as I saw the two of them I knew what they had come to say. They had the tragic news that my father had been killed. One of them took my arm for fear I might faint; but something wonderful happened. I felt the arms of the Lord around me in a way I have never experienced before in my life. I remember the officer asking, "Where's your mother?" She was down in the basement doing the washing and singing away. He asked me to go and get the next door neighbour to come in and comfort my mother. I did so, but the neighbour went into hysterics and my mother ended up comforting her. I remember my mother in the basement with the two men. They told her the bad news that her husband had been killed. She replied, "The Lord has given and the Lord has taken away, blessed be the name of the Lord." There wasn't a finger of accusation pointed at the Lord and the singing didn't stop.'

The body of Richard's father was brought home. Different people came to visit. They came from all over the British Isles and from the Republic of Ireland. Richard's family were able to tell them of the Lord who was present in even the worst situations. A group of men came from the Fire Station where he was in charge. They all went up into the room and Richard said, 'Look lads, all stand and I'll pray for us all.' He put one arm round one man and another arm round another and prayed, thanking the Lord for his father and his influences on each and every one of those men, and asked the Lord that one day each of his father's colleagues would come to know Christ. There was one man in particular who for the first time realized that he needed to trust the Saviour.

Richard's mother woke up in the middle of the night a day or so before the funeral and felt the Lord was asking her and the family to sing at the funeral. She remembered how they had been singing for many years when everything was going well, so why should they cease just because tragedy had struck? She put it to the family. Richard asked his mother what piece they would sing at the funeral. He went to his father's room and there was a music book with a marker in it at the song, 'All your anxiety all your care, bring to the Saviour's feet and leave it there'. As a family they sang that at the funeral service. God was present with them. The church was absolutely

packed out with many fire officers and others who
had grown to love his father over the years.
Richard met a man recently who said, 'To my
dying day I will never forget that funeral service.'

Richard reflects on this and asks: 'When I die
how will I be remembered? Will I be remembered
as a gossip or as one who influenced others for the
Lord? I believe my father was one who influenced
others for the Lord. When he died and went to be
with the Lord in heaven the headlines in the local
newspaper were, "The Good Samaritan". When I
look at that, that is how I would like to leave this
scene of time, being an influence to others and
leading them to the Saviour. My father is in heaven
today, not because he was good, but because all his
sin has been paid for by the Lord Jesus on the
cross. Christ alone can make a person fit for
heaven. My father trusted in that, and now I want
everyone to know this same good news.

'Just before my father died he bought a plaque
which said,

There is only one life that will soon be past,
And only what's done for Christ will last.

'I remember the Lord saying to me very clearly
through it all, "You've only one life, Richard. It
will soon be past and what are you going to do with
it?" I was brought face to face with the Lord and I
said, "Lord, you can take my life and use it." The

Lord took my life and I was ultimately led into full-time Christian work with Every Home Crusade. I believe that were it not for the death of my father I would not be in full-time Christian work today.'

6

Teenage Tragedy
The Story of Paul Kobryn

Are not two sparrows sold for a copper coin? Yet not one of them falls to the ground apart from your Father's will. But the very hairs of your head are numbered. Do not fear therefore, you are of more value than many sparrows. (Matt 10:29-31)

'My earliest memories are of being taken away from my mother by police or social workers. Sometimes the fire service had to break down the doors to get to me. The social worker had to wrench me from my mother. She was suffering from a severe mental illness at the time, and was unable to look after me,' says Paul Kobryn as he reflects on his life which by any standard has not been easy.

Paul was moved to a Children's Home where he was to spend much of his childhood. He made frequent visits home but they were very traumatic because of his mother's erratic behaviour. Eventually, he was made a Ward of Court for his own protection. His schooling was affected so he fell behind his classmates. He was unable to concentrate because of all his emotional problems, so at the age of nine he was sent to a special school.

When he was twelve, Paul asked to be fostered by a family. This was a big step for him because he was frightened of his mother's reaction. She accepted it, however, and Paul was introduced to his future foster parents, Ray and Pat, and began to spend weekends with them. 'Already God was working in my situation,' says Paul. Although at the time he didn't know it, Pat and Ray were Christians and had been praying that the Lord would lead them to the right child to foster. At the same time, the Christian head of the Children's Home had been praying for a Christian foster home for him.

'When I was in the Children's Home we were sent to Bible Class,' Paul continues. 'One of the things I was looking forward to when I was fostered was not having to go any more; but to my dismay, on the first Sunday with Ray and Pat, off we all went to church! I wasn't at all happy with this, and found it very boring.' Pat and Ray already had two children of their own, but the family quickly accepted Paul. He found it strange that the home was so 'open'. Money would be left lying around because there was a basic trust and honesty. As a family they shared everything openly, not only their material possessions but also their feelings and problems.

However, over the four years of sharing in

family life, Paul found it hard to adjust. He says
that he was stubborn and had many arguments
with his foster parents. He didn't feel that they
gave him enough time, and when he looked at
other children with their real parents, he felt left
out. People he knew, even Christians, had
different and varying standards and he found this
very confusing.

During his first year with his foster parents Paul
debated with Pat and Ray about their Christian
faith. He found it difficult to see their point of view
on issues such as the creation of the world or even
forgiveness of sin. Ultimately Paul became so
uneasy and worried about the problems and
difficulties in his life that he decided to turn to God
for help. He describes what happened on Sunday,
January 16th 1983, at a Church service in Alton,
Hampshire. 'It was an unforgettable day. I committed my life to Christ. My reaction was
incredible. I was so excited. I immediately bought
a new Bible. I had previously found the Bible had
no meaning for me, but after that step of
commitment, it came to life. It meant something
to me. I began to understand it more and to see
how it applied to my everyday life. I started to
realize all that Jesus had done for me by his death
on the cross to take the punishment for my sins.
Church too became a pleasure, not a duty. I got
involved in church activities, Mission Solent and
United Beach Missions, which I really loved.' But
somehow it didn't last. 'I still had many problems
because of all the upheavals in my life and my lack
of a trusting family background. I found it

difficult to adjust to my foster family, and very hard to trust them or the Lord. It was hard to ask for anything, even such a simple thing as a packet of crisps. I would just help myself. It would never occur to me to give advance warning of a weekend Scout camp. I didn't mean to hurt the feelings of my foster parents, but I was used to keeping myself to myself, relying on my own company. Gradually things began to change. I became more involved in Scouts and less concerned about Christian things and following God's way for my life. Pat and Ray were thinking of moving away, and I was discussing with my social worker the possibility of a flat of my own and a Youth Training Scheme course on child care. I booked into a three week Scout camp for underprivileged Asian children from the East End of London and ruled out Beach Missions. I was determined to go to the camp and God wasn't going to stop me!'

Paul felt that he himself had been hurt so much by adults and that children ought to have their rights. His inner rebellion was growing as he started to do things he knew he ought not to. His spiritual life and the joy he had experienced in Christ were waning.

It was during this period of a spiritual decline, whilst on the way to sixth form college, that Paul was hit by a car. It was June 11th, 1986, a very wet and dark Wednesday morning. He was cycling up a busy road preparing to turn right when a car whose driver did not see him hit him from behind. He was thrown back and then somersaulted forward. His neck was broken.

But God had not forsaken him. Within minutes four significant people were on the scene of the accident — a nurse, a man who knew his foster mother, a policeman and a Christian friend who was able to pray for the Lord's help in the situation.

'When I came round in the hospital I found I was paralyzed from the shoulders down. I have no recollection of the first traumatic week but just hazy memories of seeing people's feet when I was upside down on the Striker frame. Because of the shock my main worries were what had happened to my bike and my clothes!' says Paul. 'Then followed a year in a Spinal Injuries Unit. I had three major operations on my neck, which were so serious that for a while my life was in danger. I had many questions and feared that, like Job in the Old Testament, God would allow further calamities to befall me. However, John, a Christian physiotherapist at the unit, was a source of enormous support and encouragement to me, and I gradually recovered my strength. When I was transferred to a recovery unit he arranged for me to attend a nearby church where I received a warm and loving welcome. Friends wrote and visited, many prayed, and gradually light began to shine at the end of the tunnel. I now have adapted accommodation in a bungalow. I am still in a wheelchair and paralyzed as before, but am now regularly committed to a college course, to Christian work through Young Life, and when possible, to the Scouts who have been faithful friends to me throughout my treatment. Transport is always a problem for me, and I have to rely on friends for lifts, or on the transport provided by the unit. Through it all, I've grown spiritually and learned to trust God more. He has given me a sense of peace and purpose and I have been able to share my faith with people and in places to which before I would never have had access. I am praying that in the future perhaps God will enable me to help in establishing some sort of ministry for the disabled to help to share the hope and new life which become real to me.'

Needless to say, Paul has often wondered why this has happened, but it is not a question which troubles him now. As he will tell anyone who asks, the Christian life is not immune from bad circumstances. Hanging in Paul's room is a plaque which says that God does not promise sun without rain, but he does give grace and strength to meet all needs. He says, 'I accept God's will, even though I don't have any explanations. Frankly, I deserve far worse because of all my sin.'

Paul finds it hard when he sees other Christians for whom life seems so smooth and easy, but he gladly testifies to the fact that God has drawn much closer to him.

Paul has no glib answers, but he does try to be honest. He says that life is 'hard work now,' and 'I don't enjoy it like I used to. It is a hassle,' but he also says that he has realized that 'physical life isn't important'. He feels that people foolishly rush about doing this and that, not realizing they could die at any moment, when Christ will want to know how real was our life with him and whether we lived for eternity.

'If it wasn't for wanting to spread the gospel, and proclaim that Christ died for our sins according to the Scriptures, and that he was buried and that he rose again the third day . . . I would want to go to heaven today. But even now, though all this life is a spiritual battle, the Lord stays by me. He speaks so clearly to me. I trust him for everything — I have no other choice. As God says in Jeremiah 23:23, "I am a God near at hand . . . and not a God afar off".'

7

A Marriage Made in Heaven? The Story of David and Sandra Humphreys

The LORD is a refuge for the oppressed, a stronghold in times of trouble.   *(Ps 9:9)*

David and Sandra are in their early forties. Until he took early retirement Dave was a policeman in the Staffordshire Police Force.

They met when Dave was on the beat in Stafford town centre about 1965. Sandra was working at the local Town Clerk's office and delivering mail to the police station on a regular basis.

Dave had been brought up in the country. His father worked in the timber yard on the local estate. Though he went to a good school, he feels he wasted his opportunity to learn as he spent most of his time playing cricket, representing both his school and his county. As his father was also caretaker of the local men's club, Dave used to go there and play billiards. He left school at seventeen with only one 'O' level — in English Language. He applied to join the Police Cadets, without any clear reason for doing so.

Sandra and Dave knew each other for two years and were married in 1967. At the beginning everything was fine. Sandra was out working and earning money and they were able to go out and enjoy themselves. They didn't appear to have any problems at that stage.

Problems started though when their first daughter, Kerry, was born in 1970. At first Dave was a proud and doting father but that didn't last. By the time their second daughter, Joanne, was born in 1973 he spent much time away from home. In the summer he played cricket which involved socializing and drinking after the matches. In the winter he would go out playing cribbage and darts which again involved a lot of drinking.

After Joanne was born Sandra suffered from post-natal depression. They lacked money because Sandra wasn't working, and there were now two little ones to feed and care for. Dave could not cope with her depression and so a vicious circle developed. The more depressed Sandra got, the more Dave went out; the more Dave went out the more depressed Sandra became.

Sandra had no one to talk to except a best friend who was also suffering from depression. This fed their depression rather than solving any of their problems.

Sandra was brought up without a father. When she was suffering from depression her doctor said to her that he felt she was perhaps being unfair to Dave because she was expecting him to be both a father and a husband to her. He did not feel that Dave was able to do that.

Throughout all the difficulties Dave would never admit that he had a problem. He had, of course, seen other people with problems. Anyone who was drinking as regularly as he was had got a problem, but at the same time Dave did not feel addicted to drink. He always said he was not going out for the drink but just to enjoy the company.

In 1975 Sandra's sister-in-law, who was Kerry's godmother asked if Kerry could go to Sunday School. Her sister-in-law was a Christian and took very seriously the vows she had made at Kerry's christening. She asked if Sandra would take Kerry to Sunday School at the local Baptist church down the road from where they lived. At first Sandra used to take Kerry to the Sunday School and come back home again. After a few weeks the minister's wife asked if she would like to stay for the service. She did, and enjoyed it very much. She was impressed with the friendliness of the people who were there, though at that time she was still very depressed and was on anti-depressant tablets. Dave wasn't bothered about her going as long as it did not affect him. Gradually she progressed from going once a month to going every week.

Some time later Sandra and a friend decided that they needed to have a night out so they went to a local night club where Cliff Richard was appearing. In the middle of this concert Cliff stopped the proceedings and gave his testimony about how he had become a Christian, and then sang two Christian songs. The second song had a great impact on Sandra. It was called, 'Such is the Mystery', and spoke about all the free things that God gives to everybody in creation. At the end of it Cliff stood with his arms outstretched in the shape of a cross with a red spotlight on him. It really affected her as she felt that if he could stand up in that smoky atmosphere, with people drinking and swearing, and say what Jesus had done for him, it must mean something real.

Later she spoke to her brother who is a Christian. Over the years he had spent a lot of time with Sandra and the girls, particularly on Sundays. They just sat in the house and talked, and at that stage Sandra asked what a Christian was and what she had to do to become a Christian. 'I felt at that stage that I really wanted to know Jesus as my Saviour. It had clearly made such a difference in Cliff Richard's life. He could actually stand up publicly in difficult places and tell his story, and I felt it meant such a lot to him. I wanted that for myself,' Sandra says.

'My brother explained the gospel to me and said that I needed to pray and repent of my sins. Christ had died, paying for my sins so I could be forgiven. I had to ask the Lord Jesus into my heart, which I did. But I don't think anything dramatic happened at that stage, and I didn't really feel any different except that I did start to read my Bible, and I did pray and thought about God an awful lot.'

However, the real turning point came about June 1977. Sandra tells the story:

'Dave had been playing in an all-day cricket

match. He went out quite early in the morning and he didn't arrive home until the early hours of the following morning. When he came into the bedroom he was obviously drunk and, when I spoke to him, it became apparent that he didn't even know where he was and that he could not remember driving home.

He had been drunk on occasions before but he had never actually driven the car in that state. He didn't know how he had got home and that made me very angry, and I said it was totally irresponsible to be driving a car in that condition. He could have killed somebody. We ended up having a blazing row. We had had rows before, hundreds of them. I could not stand drinking, and every time he came in smelling of beer it made me angry; but this really affected me quite badly, and during this row he actually hit me, which he had never done before. It was quite violent in that I actually landed on the floor and hit my head. By this time Kerry and Joanne were both awake and all three of us were crying, so I got them into bed with me and pleaded with Dave to go and sleep in one of the girls' beds and to leave us alone. He ranted and raved a bit and kept storming round the bed and shouting things at me about how I was mad and needed to be put in a mental home. Things were getting worse and I cried out to God. I just said, "God if you are there please help me now . . . I need your help now." Suddenly a tremendous sense of peace came over me and I stopped crying and became quite rational and just talked to Dave, and he went out and got into one of the girls' beds.

Then I put my arms around the girls and they
stopped crying, and we went to sleep. It was
something I had never been able to do before.
When we had had rows previously, I would lie
awake for most of the night very upset and sometimes very angry as well, but this time I felt this
wonderful peace and knew that Jesus had come
into my life. I felt absolutely marvellous the next
day. I had no effects at all from the bump on the
head or anything else. I actually went and told the
minister's wife what had happened and I told my
brother, and they were as convinced as I was that
the Lord had indeed come into my life.'

At first Sandra felt that their marriage was over.
She did not feel she had any love left for Dave.
They seemed to want totally different things out of
life and she believed that things had become so bad
between them that nothing could make any
difference. She told this to the minister's wife who
said to Sandra, 'Oh no, I am sure the Lord does
not want you to leave Dave. I know it is going to be
difficult, but we will meet together and we will
pray for him and we will see what happens.'
Gradually, over the times of prayer that they had
together Sandra felt that the Lord would save
Dave, but secretly she thought it would be when
he was a lot older.

Dave was very sceptical about Christians and
very anti-Christian. Gradually Sandra dropped
little things about God into the conversation. Dave
could see that there was a difference in her. There
was less aggravation and argument. Her attitude
was different. Eventually Dave came to the point

where he realized he was not happy in himself and seeing the change in Sandra he wanted to experience it. He says, 'I saw more of a contentment in her life and I was not contented. I was attracted to it to such an extent that even though in my own heart I would have wanted to resist it, I could not. I went to church and I was quite impressed. I do not remember anything of what I now know as "the gospel" but I can remember the friendliness of the people there. I can remember singing hymns that I had not sung before that seemed to be a happier sort of hymn than I had experienced in church as a child. In 1 Peter chapter 3 in the Bible it speaks about wives making an impression on their husbands, not by their appearance but by the way they are, and that was what impressed me. At that time I did not consider myself a sinner in need of forgiveness, but I saw something that I thought would make me happier, and it was something I wanted to pursue.'

It was about twelve months after Sandra had been converted that Dave himself trusted Christ. 'I knew enough to know that I had to ask Jesus into my life, I can remember walking along the road and being upset about my situation, and I can remember just simply asking Jesus to come into my life and that was it. I came home and told Sandra what I had done,' Dave recalls. He had put his trust in the crucified and risen Christ.

It made an immediate difference but there were difficulties to overcome because the situation within the family was still the same. Dave felt challenged about how he was using his life and

money. He stopped smoking as much for health
reasons as for anything else, but as soon as he
stopped he found he had no desire to smoke again.
Some Christian friends talked to him about drink.
They didn't say he should not go out for a drink,
but asked if he really felt that the public house was
where he ought to be. 'Would you rather spend
your time with those people than with your own
family?' From that time on he never went out on a
Friday night again.

In 1978 Dave and Sandra were baptized
together. Dave says, 'As I look back, and perhaps I
did not realize it then, the Lord did not only save
me, he saved our marriage, because I am sure that
if I had not been saved we would not be married
now. I would have lost my wife and my family.
That would have all been gone and destroyed, I am
convinced of that.

'One of the first tests of our faith was that we
prayed about having another child and felt that it
was right to do that. Sandra became pregnant very
quickly and had a trouble-free pregnancy until the
fifteenth week when she miscarried. We were
devastated by that and could not understand why
God had let that happen when that was the baby
we had prayed for.'

'But there again,' says Sandra, 'God met me in a
very special way when I had the miscarriage.
Although we might not know the reasons for these
things happening, there is a reason for it, and I
believe the Lord has enabled me to talk to other
people I have since met who have had miscar-
riages. He blessed us with Gemma the following

year and she has been a very special joy to all of us. We had two daughters during the non-Christian part of our marriage and it was nice to have a daughter within a Christian marriage, and that was quite important. We thank God that his blessing has been upon us and that our three daughters are Christians and have been saved from the pain and misery that we brought upon ourselves.'

Both Dave and Sandra are involved in their local church. Do they ever argue now?

'Oh, no, never! Never let the sun go down on your anger! The sun has gone down on my anger on odd occasions,' says Dave, 'but when we have differences of opinion we are able to deal with them, and we know that the Lord is in the midst of our family. We know he is active in our lives, we know he is there and when they arise we are able to overcome our difficulties.'

8

Family Handicaps
Philip and Catherine Campbell's Story

*When you pass through the waters, I will be with you;
and through the rivers, they shall not overflow you.
When you walk through the fire, you shall not be
burned, nor shall the flame scorch you. For I am the
Lord your God.*   *(Isa 43:2–3)*

'Mr and Mrs Campbell, we are very sorry but your
little daughter will never be normal. She is very
severely handicapped. Did you not realize that?'

We can imagine how Phil and Catherine felt that
day, sitting facing the paediatrician when their
daughter Cheryl was only seven months old. It
seemed that the bottom had dropped out of their
world. Everything until then had been fine.
Catherine was a qualified nurse and midwife,
Philip was a full-time evangelist with the Evangeli-
zation Society. They had been married in August
1977 and were very happy. They prayed together
about every situation. In fact, during the preg-

nancy preceding the birth of Cheryl, Philip and
Catherine prayed daily that their child would be
God's child knowing and loving Christ as Saviour.
Yet here they were sitting in a doctor's surgery
having all their dreams and hopes for that child
shattered.

Cheryl, born in August 1979, was their first
child and the first grandchild in their families. At
first they could not believe what they were
hearing. Looking back they would say that despite
the initial shock, they were in the centre of God's
will — 'Everything that comes to us is Father-
filtered', quotes Catherine. Their world had not
come to an end as they had at first feared. But that
realization did not come easily.

Catherine explains her feelings.

'I went to the physiotherapist and worked with
Cheryl every day. Men of God laid hands on her
and prayed over her. But it didn't make any
noticeable difference and I started to shut God out.

'I remember going to a monthly Bible study and
hearing about the way we build walls around
ourselves and exclude God. I just broke down and
cried. I realized that God couldn't help me until I
had taken down the walls that I had built round
myself. I prayed to God, "I need you and want you
to help me." The peace that came into the room
was as if it was flooded. I was still hurting. Cheryl
still didn't sit up, but I had the peace and help of
God to cope with the problems.

'I thought everything was going to be all right
after that. My relationship with God was mended.
But one day in church the minister said, "You

have no right to question what God brings into your life." I sat there fuming — really angry — thinking, "How dare you say that? You have two perfectly normal children. You don't know what it's like to be told your daughter is never going to be like other children." But then we started to sing,

> It will be worth it all when we see Jesus,
> It will be worth it all when we see Christ.
> One glimpse of his dear face
> All sorrow will erase.
> So bravely run the race
> Till we see Christ.

and God broke down the bitterness in my heart as I realized once more that God had it under control.'

Towards the end of Cheryl's second year and after months of nursing her through a bad attack of measles, Catherine was worn out emotionally and physically but she put her hopes in a visit to an eye specialist.

'I was trying to be positive. I was really confident that her eyesight would be OK.'

But a brief examination from the specialist shattered Catherine's hopes. 'The eye centres of her brain are not developed,' he announced, leaving Catherine stunned.

'I just sat and cried. I felt as if I was all alone in the world.

'I said, "That's it God, we're finished. I don't want any more to do with you. We'll look after our daughter ourselves. We don't need you!" '

Catherine felt she could take no more — Cheryl could not walk or talk, she had epilepsy and a twisted back, but now her mother was told that she would never be able to see. She was diagnosed as suffering from microcephaly. As she pushed Cheryl in her pushchair everybody seemed to brush by her. She walked through the rain to the car where Philip was waiting.

'I yelled at him. "That's it. God doesn't care. I just can't take any more".'

Philip didn't reply, but as Catherine sat in the back of the car, 'It was as if God whispered in my ear, "Fear not, I am with you."

'It was just as if someone was talking to me; like a big bucket of peace being poured over me. God was saying he was with me.'

A Bible verse that had been precious to her as a teenager came back to her: 'Fear not, for I have redeemed you; I have called you by my name; you are Mine. When you pass through the waters, I will be with you; and through the rivers they shall not overflow you. When you walk through the fire you shall not be burned, nor shall the flame scorch you' (Isa 43:1–2). That has been the key lesson Catherine and Philip have learned through Cheryl — not that God takes away all their problems and difficulties, but he is right there with them in the crisis. He gives them peace on the inside although life on the outside doesn't always seem to make sense.

Should we not learn to trust Him
Who knoweth all things best?

> And then whate'er befalls us
> We'll still have peace and rest.

'In fact God has used Cheryl to introduce us to others with whom we can share the love of Christ. She has drawn out love from many and opened opportunities to share with others in similar circumstances,' says Philip.

In November 1981 Philip and Catherine had a baby boy, Paul. He was perfectly normal. Three and a half years later in July 1985 they had a third child, a baby daughter. There was real elation that now they had a 'normal' boy and girl. They were so delighted in her that they named her Joy. They were told that she was well and healthy and strong.

But after about six weeks, the paediatrician told Catherine that Joy had the same condition as Cheryl and that things would probably go the same way that they had with Cheryl. Once again the family was devastated. They cried to God, 'Why? What more is there to learn? We have learned so much through Cheryl. Why do we need to learn this again?' It was hard to see God's purposes and plans.

Their church loved them and supported them through this trying period. But after the initial shock wore off the pressure mounted. People prayed and they prayed, and God answered; but they still felt a great lack of confidence in themselves. Two handicapped girls under the age of six were more than they could cope with. Catherine didn't find it easy to share everything with others. She realized she had to seek the Lord herself. Again Scripture verses and Christian poems were very helpful. Catherine keeps a book of all the things which have been a blessing to her. She often opens it and reminds herself of the good which God has for her. At that time the hymn which encouraged her was:

> Oh safe to the Rock that is higher than I
> My soul in its conflicts and sorrows would fly.
> So weary, so sinful
> Thine, thine would I be.
> Thou blessed Rock of Age, I'm hiding in Thee.

Philip and Catherine have found that their Christian character has grown through all these pressures. 'Every failure is an experience to teach us something new. We need to learn to use our failures. The Bible says, "Those who wait on the Lord shall renew their strength; they shall mount up with wings like eagles; they shall run and not be weary, they shall walk and not faint." '

In December 1989 Cheryl was in hospital for a week with double pneumonia. Early one Sunday morning the telephone rang. The night sister told Philip that just moments before Cheryl had died. Philip walked back up the stairs, woke Catherine and told her that their little girl had gone Home. They were sad days. But they have hope which doesn't come with a set of easy answers. They have learned that God wants to be involved in the hurts and heart-aches of life and he doesn't stop pouring out his peace.

'It's as if I go from one hurdle to the next, but

I'm glad that I have God to help me over those hurdles. I have my weepy days, but that shows I am human,' says Catherine.

'Some say there is no hope, but Cheryl had a purpose and a quality in her life that God gave her. We saw God's plans being worked out even in her wee life.

'People don't like to think about death and heaven, but God has shown me there is so much to look forward to. Her life wasn't worthless. She had been very precious to us and I wouldn't have changed the real Cheryl.'

Philip continues, 'We are sustained knowing that Cheryl is with Christ which is far better. Down here she could not walk, but now she is walking the streets of glory. Down here she could not see, but now she is looking upon the face of Jesus. Down here she could not talk but now she is singing the praises of Christ. We could not keep going without God, he is our refuge and strength, a very present help in times of trouble. God has his purpose in all these things even though we may not see it now.'

When they sat in the funeral car on the way to the cemetery there came over them a great peace such as they had never experienced before. God met and has continued to meet them in their need.

9

Murder in the Back Yard
The Story of Beryl McConnell

> *For I am persuaded that neither death nor life, nor angels nor principalities nor powers, nor things present nor things to come nor height nor depth, nor any other created thing, shall be able to separate us from the love of God which is in Christ Jesus our Lord.*
>
> *(Rom 8:38–39).*

'I was privileged to be brought up in a home where we had the habit of going to church. At the age of 9 or 9½, as the result of a children's mission which was held at the church, I knew in my young heart that I was hearing something I wanted to know more about, and I made a commitment to the Lord Jesus Christ.' So said Beryl McConnell, widow of the Deputy-Governor of the Maze Prison who was murdered by terrorists in March, 1984. She continued, 'After the commitment I did not feel much different but there was always the desire to know more about Jesus.' Going to Sunday School led to her becoming a Sunday School teacher in an attempt to give the children something she had received, and finally at the age of 17½ she committed her life to Christ in a much more meaningful way. She began to understand the love of God and the sacrifice that he had made through the death of the Lord Jesus. The fact that the Lord Jesus had died for her, 'a pathetic sort of creature', made her believe that she could not go through life without committing herself to this God.

Beryl did not marry early in life. She wanted to be sure that she was marrying the right man and he just did not turn up until, through a complicated arrangement, Beryl was introduced to Bill. 'I think it is lovely if you can meet somebody and fall in love and get married when you are young, but I didn't meet "Mr Right". I met a girl friend of mine who met Bill through her work and had said to me, "I know somebody who would suit you," and I said, " Where is this guy?" At that stage he was working in Magilligan Prison and some months later she arranged a supper party and unknown to me, invited Bill as well as me. During the evening, I noticed that when he was actually talking there was a depth to him and he was interested in people. He seemed to have a fair amount of knowledge about a number of subjects. It also struck me that he had thought through a number of things and was very clear in his own mind where he stood on certain issues, and I thought, "Here is a guy who really knows where he is going." It was his strength of character, if you like, that really appealed to me.

'He had been brought up in a Christian home but it was in Holywood, in Northern Ireland, where he was at school and a member of the Christian Union, that he ceased to think of religion as something reserved for Sunday and became aware of what the Lord Jesus was doing in the lives of his schoolfellows. I think it was that influence which really led him to make a commitment to the Lord Jesus at that stage,' Beryl recalled.

They were married in 1979 and their marriage lasted a fortnight short of five years. They had a little girl, called Gail, who was 3½ when Bill was murdered.

It was in 1983 when 38 prisoners broke out of the Maze Prison that the final chapter in the life of Bill McConnell began. There was a huge outcry following the breakout, and Sir James Hennesey and a team of investigators were despatched to enquire how the escape had occurred. Their report (published in January 1984) made certain points about which the Governor and his staff were most unhappy and it was decided that though it had never been done before, a public reply would have to be made. Bill McConnell offered to be the spokesman and became a focal point for both local and national media. Interviews were arranged and one local radio station came to their home to make a taped recording to be broadcast on 3rd February. An ITV crew had also come from England and went to the McConnell's house. While the equipment, cameras, microphones, etc. were being set up in their home, Bill and Beryl talked very briefly. There was a lot going on, 'phones were ringing and folk were chatting; but they talked about where this could lead. Beryl said, 'You know Bill, you could lose your job. You could end up in prison if you said too much. You could break the Official Secrets Act and end up in your own prison.' Then she added, 'It could bring about your death.' She doesn't know why she said it but she just felt it was a possibility. They didn't say anything more about it but committed the situation to the Lord, saying that whatever was in the future was in the Lord's hands and they would rest secure in him.

Unknown to Beryl, the next morning, after the radio interviews had been done and the T.V. interview had been recorded, Bill went into the office and wrote a letter. It is not unusual for people in Northern Ireland to write a testamentary letter because they are doing a job of work which entails a certain amount of danger. Usually the letters ask for certain hymns to be played at funerals, or make certain arrangements for funerals. Bill didn't only leave that, but left his Christian testimony. Part of the letter reads: 'My wife, Beryl, has been supportive of all I have done. I would commend her and Gail to your keeping and prayers.

'Finally, let no one be alarmed as to my eternal security. In March 1966, I committed my life, talents, work and actions to Almighty God in sure and certain knowledge that however slight my hold upon Him may have been during my years at school, university and the prison service, His promises are sure, and His hold on me complete. Nothing can separate me from the love of God in Christ Jesus our Lord.'

He gave the letter, in a sealed envelope, to one of his Christian colleagues in the prison.

Some may feel that Bill was too casual about his personal security. He left the car outside the house, and often he did not even lock it. He had been issued with a gun and trained to use it, but did not carry it. He had been measured for a flak-jacket. He brought it home where it was put in the cloakroom and gathered dust. On one occasion Beryl said, 'You are going to have to be more careful, because there could be a car bomb one morning.' He replied, 'Look, sit down while I speak to you. I have committed my life to the Lord and I am not going to die one second before the Lord wants me to go to heaven. I don't know how I am going to die or when I am going to die. If it means I am going to die at the end of a bullet fired by a terrorist gunman, it is the way the Lord has it and I am happy with that.'

The day of Bill's murder began as a very ordinary day in their lives. It was a Tuesday morning, 6th March, 1984. Bill was having breakfast, little Gail was chattering, and Beryl went out of the house and cleaned the windows of his car, so he could jump into it and head off to work as he was always late. She then helped Bill on with his coat. They had their usual hugs and kisses and said goodbye, 'Because', as Beryl says, 'each

time he left home, either to go to work, to go to a
church or a scout meeting, we always said our
goodbyes as if it might be the last time. One never
knew when death would strike. You don't have to
be old or infirm, death can come very quickly to
young and old alike.' They then went out to the car
which was at the front of the house. Beryl noticed
things happening around the house directly across
the road from them, things that were not normal.

An elderly couple lived across the road from
them. They were not usually out and about at 8.15
in the morning but Beryl noticed that the car was
in the drive, not in the garage, and was facing
towards the street instead of away from it as it
usually would be. She thought something was
wrong. Then she saw a couple of young men
coming out of the drive and she started trying to
put answers to what was happening. 'What were
these people doing? They were not binmen — no.'
Suddenly she realized, as they started to come
across the road towards their gate, that they were
in fact carrying guns and were preparing to fire
them. Seeing that Bill was just about to be shot,
she shouted a warning to him. He turned and saw
them and then he turned away in an attempt to try
to avoid being shot. They were only a matter of
three or four yards from him when they opened
fire. Bill received a number of bullets in the head
and fell dead. He probably died instantly. The gun
was an automatic pistol and the bullets just flew
into his body. Gail was there and saw what
happened. When the bangs started she was
frightened and cried and screamed, and ran into

the house. She didn't actually see her father and
the mess that was around his body.

With bullets flying all around, and two gunmen,
Beryl was not sure whether she was going to be
killed or not. Quickly, though, the gunmen left
Bill dead on the ground and made their getaway.
Beryl realized that it was safe to get up from her
crouching position beside Bill's car. She could see
that Bill was dead. Beryl recalled that she
immediately thought, 'Well, he is in the presence
of God at last. I looked at his body and felt that it
was almost like clothing that we put on, it was the
body in which God had placed his soul, and that
that soul had gone to be with God in heaven.' Beryl
continued, 'Nobody really knows how they are
going to react when something dramatic happens.
I must say, I felt calm, I didn't dissolve into tears.
In fact I can honestly say that I never had the
feeling that I had to sit down and weep bitter tears.
I really did feel that God was with me; and Bill's
family, who are Christians, felt that strength, and
it was a visible strength because we were not bitter,
we were not sad. There was a peace. You know,
they talk about this peace beyond human understanding. It must have come from God; where else
would it have come from? It was there, it kept me
going, it allowed me to speak to people, and in fact
my heart went out to other people who probably
felt Bill's loss almost more than I did. I had been
present at his death and had come to terms with it,
but his old friends were coming to the house and
they just could not take it in, and I was actually
finding myself trying to comfort them.'

Her faith as a little girl aged nine, and re-dedication at the age of seventeen, proved real and valuable despite terrible circumstances. In fact, she would say, 'I actually think my faith is much stronger, because with the event of Bill's death, God gave me the strength that I needed to get me through those difficult days. That did not stop at any stage, it is still with me. My daughter was only 3½ and I had to look after her and bring her up. In some way I had to be supportive to my husband's parents who had lost their son, and to his sisters who had lost their brother. We all had a loss, a different sort of loss, and I know the Lord God and his strength is with me every day, and there is a peace and a joy in my heart because I have experienced what God can do in someone's life.'

Speaking of her husband's murderers, Beryl says, 'I can honestly say that none of the family has ever said a bitter word about the people involved. We, in fact, have been praying from the time of Bill's death that the people involved in his murder would in some way come to know of the saving grace that God gives. I know that some of the people involved in Bill's murder have been arrested and are in prison, some have been sentenced, and there are some who have not yet been brought to prison who are presumably walking free. Irrespective of where they are, our prayer has been that God would one day, very soon, speak to them, and that they will come to know the love of Christ and commit their lives to him. If that happened I would probably be one of the first in the queue to shake hands and to greet them as a fellow brother in the Lord. I know that Bill will be delighted to see them in heaven one day, and we just pray that those people who find themselves in prison may, through the influences of the prison chaplains or Christian prisoners (a number of prisoners in Crumlin Road Prison are Christians) or perhaps through members of the prison staff who are Christians, come to know about the Lord Jesus and feel that they could dedicate their lives to him. I would be delighted. If it takes Bill's murder to bring those people to the Lord, Bill's murder will have been well and truly worth every second of the loneliness and the pain that we have suffered.'

Just a few months before his death, Bill McConnell wrote an article for a church magazine. In it he said, 'The death of an individual at the hands of a murderer, though a tragic event, cannot be considered the ultimate tragedy. We must trust God's sovereignty in these things and thank Him for the life that has passed to eternity.'

Bill's funeral service was to be an act of praising God, not just for Bill's life, but for the fact that he had been saved through the death and resurrection of the Lord Jesus. As a family they were happy. Knowing that they had both committed their lives to the Lord, Beryl is sure that one day they will see God's face. 'It must be tremendous to enter into heaven and see at last the face of God and to see Christ beside him. It is very exciting to know that that is at the end of our earthly life' says Beryl.

10

'Til Death Us Do Part
The Story of Susan Sahl

The Lord will commend his loving kindness in the daytime. And in the night this song shall be with me — a prayer to the God of my life.   (Ps 42:8)

At the age of 26 Susan Sahl's life was turned upside down when her young husband died without any warning. Sue had been converted as a young teenager, but Martin's sudden death was to be the fiercest test of her faith. Although it is still early days, she tells her poignant story and explains how she is beginning to come to terms with her tragedy.

'One Autumnal day, during my final year at Leeds University, I wandered pensively along a deserted street kicking up the fallen leaves. As I scrunched along I began to pray that by this time next year I would have met my future husband and (I added almost frivolously) "he must enjoy kicking up leaves in Autumn". Little did I know quite how significant this prayer was to become!

'Almost a year later my prayer was to be answered in a miraculous way. I was helping on a Beach Mission in Cromer and there I met a young man named Martin Sahl (known affectionately as Mart to his friends). Mart was intelligent, witty, and sincere. He had a first class degree from Cambridge, and yet his humility was second to none. As we talked I began to see the wisdom and gentleness that this young man possessed. By the end of the Mission we knew that we had not seen the last of each other!

'The following week we met in Cambridge and sitting on a bench in Emmanuel College garden we prayed together. As we finished Mart glanced at a beautiful tree above us, one small patch of which was turning amber; he looked at me and said, "I love kicking up leaves in Autumn, do you?" Well I didn't say anything to him, but I realized immediately that our relationship should be allowed to flourish!

'It was not long before we began to see each other on a regular basis. Every weekend Martin commuted from London, where he was training to be a Chartered Accountant, to Leicester University, where I had embarked upon a teacher training course. During the week we wrote to each other daily, it was a rich form of communication and a way in which we learnt to share every aspect of our lives with each other. Over the next year Mart and I spent countless hours deep in conversation, until we really felt that there was nothing which we did not know about each other.

'I don't think that Martin really needed to ask

me to marry him, as we simply couldn't ever imagine having to be apart. The following year we chose an engagement ring and arranged a trip to Cromer where God had first brought us together, and there Mart proposed to me. I said, "Yes" (of course!), and promptly burst into tears!

'The months to come were action-packed as we bought a house, decorated it, tamed the wild jungle of a garden, all whilst making copious plans for a spring country wedding. The day itself was wonderful and without a doubt it was the best day of our lives. God blessed those first months of our marriage so that we soon felt as though we had been married for ever.

'The following year our happiness was to be impinged on by several major things. Amongst them was the death of my grandmother and the impending death of my friend who was suffering from a brain tumour. Mart and I spent hours discussing the subject of death and how we felt about it. It was during this time that the economic recession deepened, and Martin found himself facing the prospect of redundancy. This caused us a great deal of pain and we were forced to look carefully at our finances. Mart was able to plan how we could survive on my salary. Little was I to know quite how significant these seemingly unfair events were to be in terms of preparing me for the tragedy which lay ahead.

'As Christmas 1991 approached, we made arrangements to see as many of our family and friends as we could. We spent Christmas Day at my family home in Hertfordshire and then travelled to Dorking to spend time with Martin's family. As the 27th of December drew to a close we said good-bye to Martin's parents as they were due out early the following morning, and retired happily to bed. At about 5.20 a.m. I was woken suddenly by Mart having a nightmare. I flicked on the bedside light and called out his name whilst shaking him by the shoulder, but he continued to thrash around, making a strange groaning noise. I knew instantly that something was wrong. Praying as I ran, I dashed into his sister's room for help, when we returned Mart had stopped thrashing around. Together we put him into the recovery position and Deborah ran to awaken their parents and call for an ambulance. I sat on the bed next to Mart, by now his breathing pattern had changed, he was not breathing as frequently as he should have been, then I heard one long expulsion of air, and Mart's body went limp. At that moment Martin's parents rushed in. We frantically tried to find a pulse, but there was none! Immediately we lifted his body to the floor and began "mouth to mouth" and pulmonary resuscitation. Despite my first aid training, nothing could have prepared me for the shock and trauma of desperately trying to resuscitate my own husband.

'After what seemed like an age, but was in fact only a few minutes, the ambulance crew arrived and took over from us. I was in a fog of confusion, so many thoughts were rushing through my mind. The heart monitor did not show a horizontal line but one with intermittent peaks and troughs, which made me wonder why Mart still appeared to be unconscious. I knew that we would have to go to the hospital, so I pulled on some clothes, and whilst they put Mart into the ambulance, I hurriedly rang my parents for moral and prayer support. My father answered the phone and I incoherently screamed, "Dad, Mart's stopped breathing and they are trying to resuscitate him. I've got to go to the hospital, please pray." What a garbled message for my poor parents to receive at 5.25 in the morning!

'I wanted to be allowed to travel with Mart but they wouldn't let me. We followed the ambulance through the freezing fog to the hospital, stopping at one point in the middle of the road as another ambulance flagged us down and brought extra medical supplies. From the roadside all I could see were Mart's feet poking out of a red blanket. I felt utterly helpless. Words failed me. I tried frantically to pray, but I found it so hard to string a coherent sentence together.

'As soon as we arrived at the hospital we were ushered into a corridor. I still wanted to be with Mart but once again I was barred from going with him. Martin's family went and sat in a small waiting room but I needed to be alone, so I sat curled up on the floor in the corridor. Numbly I prayed, biting back my tears and holding my head in utter disbelief at the awfulness of the situation. Shortly afterwards a young nurse came and told us that things looked very grim. Desperately I prayed again, "God if we can't have Mart back as he was, then will you take him and look after him; but if you do you'll have to help us!"

'About five minutes later the doctors came and told us that despite all their efforts Mart had died. I couldn't believe it. I felt shocked to the core, empty, numb, but painfully aware of the tragedy which had befallen us. When eventually I was allowed to see Mart I knew at once that this was just his earthly shell, he looked so peaceful, that I could hardly believe that he was dead. The full horror of the situation had not yet had a chance to sink in. I left the cubicle and headed towards the exit, I desperately needed space and solitude in which to pray and think things through.

'As the automatic door clicked open and I stepped outside, a feeling of stunned emptiness pervaded my very being. I stared in utter disbelief at the new day, crisp and frozen like my heart. I slumped exhaustedly beside a wall, tears were streaming down my face, quietly I began to pray, "Father you've taken the most precious thing in my life, please look after him, I feel so vulnerable, small and helpless, I desperately need your help." I sat alone in the semi-darkness until I felt strong enough to return to the hospital.

'Soon came the gruelling task of identifying the body. Through all this I simply couldn't believe that at 26, after only twenty short months of marriage I was a widow. There had been no warning; what on earth could have gone wrong to cause a healthy young person to die in his sleep? It simply doesn't cross your mind when you kiss your partner goodnight that he won't be alive in the morning!

'As dawn broke my parents arrived to be with

me and I took my Mother to the room where they
had placed Martin's body. I knew that I must
finally say good-bye to Mart's earthly shell. Gently
stroking his face and kissing his forehead I
whispered, "Good-bye my darling I love you."
Finally, I ran my hands through his thick dark hair
for the last time and turned to leave the room. My
heart was breaking, I felt desperately lonely,
wanting my life to end there and then. My heart
felt so full it physically hurt and I clutched my
chest in utter disbelief.

'Through the coming hours and days I had a
very real sense of God sustaining me. It may sound
strange, but at times I felt the tangible presence of
God's warm reassuring hand on my back. My
family and friends were marvellous, gently sup-
porting me and praying me through the acute
agony of those early days. One of the immediate
reactions I had to Mart's death was that I
completely lost the ability to sing, which for me
was awful. Those who know me will realize that
singing is an important part of my life. The first
words I was eventually able to sing were the words
to the song "Give thanks with a grateful heart".
This song, however croakily sung, was to be the
channel through which God could begin to
administer his healing love to my life.

'Painfully I began to make funeral preparations.
Eventually I decided that it was fitting that Mart's
earthly resting place should be the peaceful
Church in which we had been married the
previous year. I desperately wanted the service to
be one of thanksgiving for Martin's life as I knew

that we were not burying Martin, just his body. I felt the need for the service to be as peaceful and God-centred as possible. I wanted someone to pay a verbal tribute to Martin's life, so I prayed that God would show me who should speak during the service. To my horror he clearly said that I should! I felt weak and helpless. I had hardly slept or eaten for days, but I believed that God had spoken, and so I began to think about what I would say.

'The day of the funeral was incredibly difficult. I felt more nervous than I had done when I sat my finals, and yet I believed God's promise that he was an ever present help in trouble. Now when I was at my weakest, I relied totally upon him. He had never let me down in the past so I knew that he would somehow carry me through the difficult hours ahead.

'God's presence filled that village church. The warmth, love and support of my family and friends were really tangible. When I stood to speak, I could hardly believe that it was me talking. I really was given "a peace which passes all understanding" coupled with an inner strength, which enabled me to cope with the pressures of the day.

'It was several anguished weeks before we finally knew the cause of Martin's sudden death. The autopsy revealed that he had a floppy mitral valve which, coupled with sudden cardiac arrhythmia, had for some unknown reason caused instant and irreversible heart failure. God had called him home instantly without any suffering, graciously allowing those who loved him most to be with him at the time of his death.

'Despite my peace about Mart's eternal destiny, nothing could have prepared me for the utter desolation which I was to feel. At times my grief was almost uncontrollable. I seem to be enveloped by an all pervading emptiness, the ferocity of which I had never experienced before. I was totally unprepared for the depths of loneliness in which I would be submerged. All my hopes and dreams had been shattered into a myriad tiny pieces. Painful memories flooded back, each bearing a bitter sting of its own. It was as if all the things which had previously been most precious to me now cut like sharpened swords. I felt totally incomplete, as though a part of me had died. I had not reckoned on how often and unexpectedly this deep despair would rear its ugly head.

'The immense task ahead was simple in name but incredibly hard in practice. I somehow had to get my shattered life back on the rails. I felt weak and totally unco-ordinated, almost as if I was recovering from a general anaesthetic. It was really hard to begin to take everything in, somehow my brain did not have a compartment labelled "indescribable, unbelievable tragedy" into which all these events would neatly slot. It seemed so wrong to be a widow at twenty six. Only God could minister to the deep pain welling up within me. Each tearful torrent was followed by a deep sense of his being in control of the situation, if only I would allow him to be. In the face of real anguish, prayer seemed the only meaningful thing left in life. My relationship with God was literally a lifeline. Despite everything, my life was in his hands.

'At this time a close friend of mine had a vision of the family frantically trying to resuscitate Martin's body. Although I had not previously discussed this event with her, she was able to describe perfectly our positions in the bedroom. In her vision Martin and Jesus were standing in the room watching us, and Martin was smiling and saying, "It will be all right, won't it?" Somehow from the moment that I first realized that Martin had died, I knew that he was with God. He had become a Christian in his first year at University, and had a vibrantly strong faith. My friend's vision was tremendously reassuring to me, reaffirming my belief that Martin was safe in God's hands. In addition to confirming my belief in Martin's eternal destiny, God reassured me that my future is also in his hands.

'Quite independently from each other, several people wrote out one particular Bible verse which they believed was God's promise for me. It was, "For I know the plans I have, declares the Lord, plans to prosper you and not to harm you, plans to give you a hope and a future" (Jer 29). Somehow I began to see that there was going to be a future worth living.

'Gradually I came to realize that Martin's earthly life was not cut short but completed, therefore there must also be a purpose to my own sufferings. C S Lewis wrote that pain is God's megaphone to rouse a deaf world. In my pain I could hear God so clearly. When everything in my

life had been removed, my relationship with God
began to flourish. I had had years of half following,
half listening. Now in my darkest night Jesus was
standing holding the lamp which would light my
path, if only I would walk beside him and not head
off into the darkness alone. Through my suffering
God was speaking very clearly to me from the
Bible. This passage from the Good News Bible in
particular has been a great strength to me:

> Do not cling to events of the past, or dwell on
> what happened long ago. Watch for the new thing
> that I am going to do, it is happening already, you
> can see it now. I will make a road through the
> wilderness and give you streams of water there.
> (Isa 43:18,19)

'As time has worn on the intensity of pain has
begun to fade. At each step of the way God has
been a very present help, gently guiding me and
showing me the way ahead. He has given me a
future and a hope, healing my aching heart and
giving me the strength somehow to take another
step forward towards healing and wholeness.
'I know that I could never have survived this
year without God's help; the measure of healing in
me is remarkable, and whilst the journey still goes
on, I know that I will never walk alone.'

11

The Great Divide

One shining thread which has run through many
of the previous stories has been a certain convic-
tion that the sufferings of this present world will be
more than compensated for by the joy and glory
which are the future hope of the believer. So it is
important to ask ourselves whether we are absolutely certain that we share that future hope. For
there has been throughout history, and there is
still today, a basic divide between people. It is not
based upon sex, colour, race, economic situation
or even whether a person has suffered. It is based
upon whether someone knows the true and living
God. It is that relationship with God which
transforms the heart's deepest attitudes towards
every experience of life. There are so many things
which are denied to the unbeliever.

First, the believer has God to thank in times of
joy. This book has inevitably looked at difficulties,
but most people have times of great happiness and
joy. So who does one thank when one looks at a

beautiful sunset or enjoys a good meal or is with a dearly-loved friend? Who does one thank for the beauty and wonder of creation?

The story is told of two French revolutionaries who in 1789 boasted to a Christian that they would tear down every reminder that there is a God. 'Oh,' asked the believer, 'and what will you do about the stars?'

The Bible is full of people who found reasons to praise God. When Moses had led the people of Israel across the Red Sea and their enemies had been defeated, he proclaimed, 'I will sing to the LORD for he is highly exalted. The horse and its rider he has hurled into the sea.' After the building of the first temple in Jerusalem had been completed Solomon praised God: 'Praise be to the LORD, the God of Israel, who with his own hand has fulfilled what he promised with his own mouth to my father David.' Daniel, after his deliverance from the lions' den could say, 'My God sent his angel and shut the lions' mouths so that they did not hurt me.' The book of the Psalms is full of hymns of praise to God. In the midst of a storm at sea Paul found strength in praising God.

In our own day, Colonel James Irwin was one of only twelve men to have walked on the moon. He has written about his experiences:

> I felt very special when I looked at my footprints on the moon. The scientists said that they would be there for a million years. Looking up I could see the earth, the size of a marble. It was so beautiful and so far away, and yet, I felt strangely

at home. When our mission returned, I thanked the men who designed and built our spacecraft, those who helped to operate the systems during the flight, those fellow Americans who paid for our trip, those dear friends around the world who had prayed for our success, and I thanked God for allowing us to leave the earth and explore a portion of his heavens.

Secondly, the believer has God to turn to in time of trouble. All of us are aware that we depend on other people, yet strangely, along with this sense of dependency, those in need are conscious of a sense of alienation from other people. Just as we can approach a monarch only upon certain conditions, so too often we can approach others only when everything is right for us. We cannot share our needs with them.

There is a Russian fable which tells of a hospitable householder who used to tell the local villagers that they would be welcome at any time at his large house for food or warmth. Nobody ever came, though, because he had two large alsatians roaming round his grounds!

By contrast, Jesus Christ is available to all who come to him. He welcomed everybody, the unloved, the unlovely and the apparently unloveable. Not only the common people but the deprived, the despised, the sinful came to him and were not turned away. Indeed, he was described as the 'friend of sinners' and said of himself that he had come 'to seek and save the lost'.

Christ invites all to come to him. He said, 'Come to me, all you who labour and are heavy laden, and

I will give you rest. Take my yoke upon you and
learn from me, for I am gentle and lowly in heart,
and you will find rest for your souls. For my yoke
is easy and my burden is light' (Matt 11:28–30).
Jesus invites us to come just as we are. He doesn't
ask us to improve ourselves or make ourselves
worthy, simply to come with the needs that only he
can satisfy. The believer is one who has heard and
answered that call and knows that Jesus Christ is
the only one who can satisfy man's deepest needs.

Thirdly, the believer has God to trust in life and
death. All people have decisions to make, difficulties to face, despondency to overcome. Because he
not only died, but also rose from the dead, Jesus is
now a living, loving Saviour to all those who trust
him.

The Bible teaches us that we can cast all our care
upon him because he cares for us. We read: 'Trust
in the LORD with all your heart, and lean not on your
own understanding; in all your ways acknowledge
him and he shall direct your paths' (Prov 3:5–6).
We have seen in the stories in the preceding
chapters that however awful the circumstances
may be through which God's people have to pass,
his eye is always on the clock and on the
thermometer. He knows exactly how long and
how 'hot' our present suffering can be. For all who
trust him there is the promise of his eternal
presence. We have the promise of Jesus: 'I am with
you always, even to the end of the age' (Matt
28:20). Again, we have God's promise: 'I will not
leave you nor forsake you' (Jos 1:5). He goes
before his people and is behind them and beside

them. He is beneath them and above them and has
promised to abide with all who trust him.

The Christian has someone who can ensure his
eternal future. The Bible teaches us that after
death there is judgment. The God who made me
has an absolute right to welcome me to heaven or
sentence me to an eternal hell. To save me from
that hell I need someone who can deal with my
past. For it is sin which will keep me from heaven
and condemn me to hell. Sin is breaking God's
commandments; it is falling short of all that God
is; it is not loving God with all my heart, mind,
soul and strength and not loving my neighbour as
myself. All sin is firstly and foremostly against
God, therefore it is his forgiveness that I need.
James Simpson who discovered chloroform was to
say that the greatest discovery of his life was that
he was a sinner in need of a Saviour. Jesus Christ is
the perfectly qualified Saviour. He did not need
forgiveness for himself because he never sinned.
But when he was on the cross, dying as a common
criminal, God was in Christ reconciling the world
to himself. Jesus was dying the death of us all, for
our sin was laid on him. He was providing the one
and only way to forgiveness and a relationship with
the true and living God.

It is because Jesus on the cross dealt with our
past sins and that three days later he rose from the
dead, that he can deal with our future. Life here on
earth is both temporary and short. According to an
old fable, a man made an unusual agreement with
Death. He told the grim reaper that he would
willingly accompany him when the time came to

die but on one condition — that Death would send a messenger well in advance to warn him. Weeks turned to months and months into years. Then one bitter winter evening, as the man sat alone thinking about all his worldly possessions, Death suddenly entered the room and tapped him on the shoulder. The man was startled and cried out in despair: 'You're here so soon and without warning! I thought we had an agreement.' Death replied: 'I've more than kept my part. I've sent you many messengers. Look at yourself in the mirror and you'll see some of them.' As the man complied, Death whispered, 'Notice your hair, once it was thick and black; now it is thin and white. Look at the way you turn your head to listen to my voice because you can no longer hear well. Observe how close you must get to the mirror in order to see yourself clearly. Yes, I've sent my messengers through the years. I've kept my part of the bargain. It is too bad that you did not keep yours. I'm sorry that you're not ready for me but the time has come to leave.'

Someone has mathematically calculated a schedule that compares the average lifetime with a single day, beginning at 7 am. If your age is:

15, the time is 10.25 am
25, the time is 12.42 pm
35, the time is 3.00 pm
45, the time is 5.16 pm
55, the time is 7.34 pm
65, the time is 9.55 pm
75, the time is 11.00 pm

Christ has tasted death for each one of us and
has conquered the grave. This very day, if you will
turn from your sin in repentance and by faith trust
him to be your Lord and Saviour, he will forgive
you and come to live with you. Jesus said: 'And the
one who comes to me I will by no means cast out.'

When you trust Christ not only does he cleanse
the past but as you serve and obey him you will
find that he guides your future. Many have found
that praying in words similar to those below has
helped them in the act of putting their trust in
Christ. Will you pray like this now?

> Heavenly Father, I confess my sin to you and
> want to repent of it. Please forgive me. I trust
> Christ as my Sin-Bearer, my Saviour, my Lord
> and my Friend. Help me to grow to become a
> strong Christian. Thank you for loving me. I pray
> in Jesus' name. Amen.

If you are sincere and serious you will have peace
with God and throughout life you can enjoy the
peace of God, and one day enjoy the eternal peace
which God has promised to all his own.